We Love Ballet!

By Jane Feldman

Special thanks to Suzanne Osterberg, Danielle Pierce, Kate Thomas, Diane Grumet, and everyone at Steps on Broadway NYC, and to our ballet dancers and their supportive parents: Ursula, Norma, Megan, Bridget, Phoebe, Christian, Zoe, Clil, Fiona, Kaili, and both Nicoles. Thanks to Capezio and Puppet Workshops for the wonderful ballet costumes.

A Random House PICTUREBACK® Book

Random House 🏠 New York

Library of Congress Control Number: 2004101258
ISBN: 0-375-82831-1
www.randomhouse.com/kids
Printed in the United States of America   First Edition   10 9

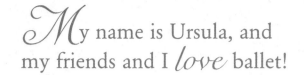

My name is Ursula, and my friends and I *love* ballet!

This is my family. We are always on the go.

I dance everywhere. I dance to school. I dance to the park. And, of course, I dance to ballet class!

Miss Suzanne is my ballet teacher.
My good friends Norma and Megan
are in her class with me.

Miss Suzanne teaches us to have fun and always do our best. First we learn the five basic positions of the feet in ballet. When we put our heels together in first position, Miss Suzanne says, "Use your imagination and picture a slice of pie between your feet."

First Position   **Second Position**   **Third Position**   **Fourth Position**   **Fifth Position**

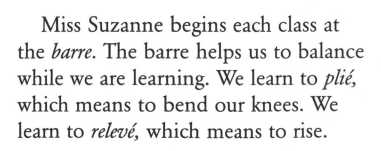

Miss Suzanne begins each class at the *barre*. The barre helps us to balance while we are learning. We learn to *plié*, which means to bend our knees. We learn to *relevé*, which means to rise.

Megan and I love to jump
and leap. Look, our feet aren't
even touching the ground!

In ballet, it's very important to warm up your muscles so you don't hurt yourself. After we do exercises at the barre, we do floor stretches. *Reach* right! *Reach* left! *Reach* and touch your toes!

Miss Danielle helps Miss Suzanne teach our class. Here she's showing Norma how to do a *passé*.

Miss Suzanne is always there to help us. She has special ways of saying things so we remember different moves. She says, "Reach for the stars, Bridget!"

In ballet, you *must* have good posture. Miss Suzanne says, "Sit up straight and make your necks long like a giraffe's!"

Shoe check! It is important to make sure your shoes are tied just right. Not too loose and not too tight. You don't want to trip.

Now we are ready to cross the floor. We all stand in a line like a choo-choo train. Miss Suzanne sets stars and circles on the floor.

When we get to a star, we have to leap high. When we get to a circle, we have to freeze like a statue!

Dancing across the floor gives us a chance to learn our music and work on the steps that we will use in our big recital.

Sometimes we go across the floor in pairs. Miss Suzanne says, "Work together, class!" We cooperate and raise our hands to ask questions, just like in school.

It's fun to dance together!

We have lots of girls in the class, but boys take ballet, too. Ballet dancers have to be very strong. I saw a ballet on television where a male dancer lifted the female dancer high above his head. That takes years of practice!

Ballet improves strength, balance, and footwork, which are important in all sports. Miss Danielle told us that lots of football players take ballet!

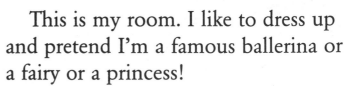

This is my room. I like to dress up and pretend I'm a famous ballerina or a fairy or a princess!

It's fun to make my own costumes. Mom lets me use ribbons and sparkles.

Sometimes when I am feeling very silly, I put my tutu on my head.

I love when my mom and I cuddle up and read fairy tales before bedtime. A lot of ballets are based on fairy tales, like *Sleeping Beauty* and *Swan Lake*.

I can't wait to get out of bed today because we are going to the ballet store! We are buying new slippers for my recital. I get to try on sparkly costumes, too!

Mom helps me pick out a pair of slippers just right for me. She tries on toe shoes and goes up on *pointe*, like she used to when she was a dancer. I wish I could go up on my tippy-toes like her, but it takes years to make your feet strong enough. Ballet can be hard work.

At last it's time for our recital. Miss Suzanne helps us get ready backstage. We get to put on our beautiful costumes, and makeup, too!

Finally, we get to show our parents what we have been learning all year. We are all so proud when the music ends and the audience claps!

We Love Ballet!

Sometimes I watch Miss Danielle and Miss Suzanne practice. I love to dream about the day when I'll be able to dance like them. I don't know whether I'll grow up to be a professional dancer or a teacher, but there's one thing I do know: I *love* ballet.